GOD
LOVES YOU!

A Book to Read with Your Child

Written by Michele Hayes-Grisham

Illustrated by Sheila Preston-Ford

LifeRich Publishing is a registered trademark of The Reader's Digest Association, Inc.

LifeRich Publishing books may be ordered through booksellers or by contacting:

LifeRich Publishing
1663 Liberty Drive
Bloomington, IN 47403
www.liferichpublishing.com
1 (888) 238-8637

ISBN: 978-1-4897-1048-2 (sc)
ISBN: 978-1-4897-1049-9 (hc)
ISBN: 978-1-4897-1047-5 (e)

Print information available on the last page.

LifeRich Publishing rev. date: 12/06/2016

To all God's children:
It doesn't matter what age you are!

To learn more about God and to gain a
deeper understanding of the love He has
for us, please read the endnotes.

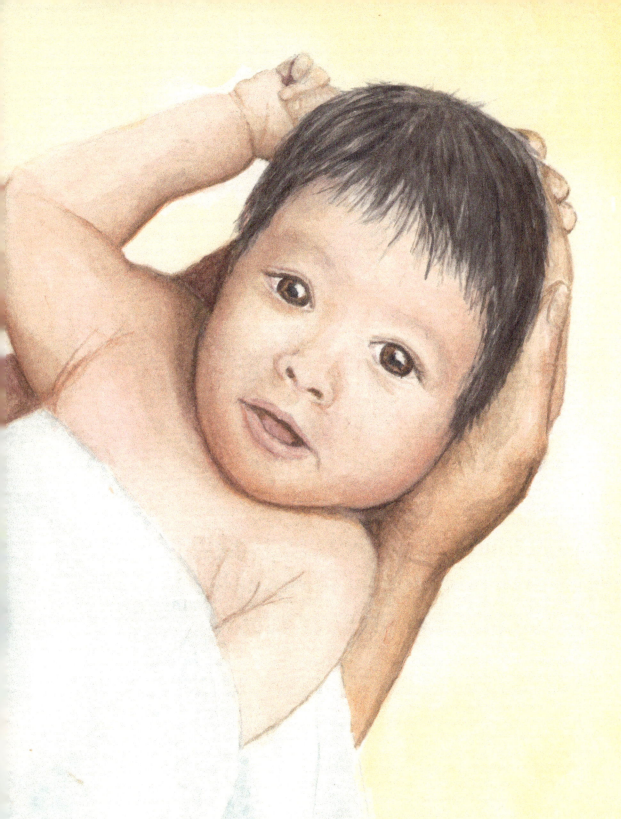

Before you were born, God loved you! God made you and He watches over you every minute. God put goodness, love, gifts, and talents inside you.

It doesn't matter if you are a boy or a girl, short or tall, weak or strong or what color your skin is; God made you and He loves you!

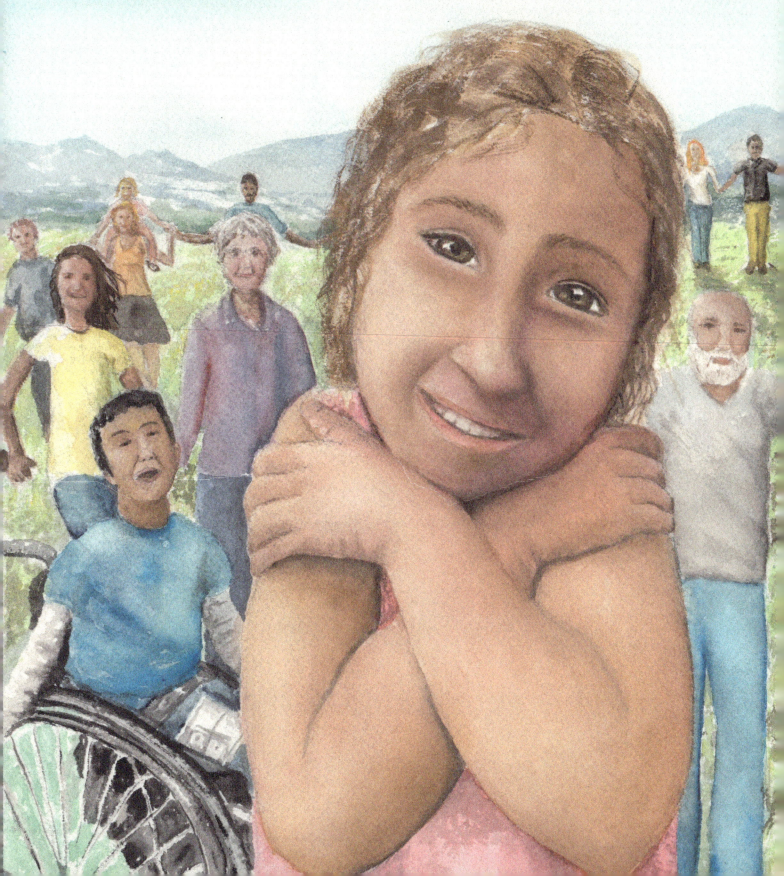

God made each person different. There are no two people exactly alike. There are even differences between twins.

Some people are full of energy and loud.
Some people are shy and quiet — and
God loves us all!

God gave us a book to teach us the best way to live. This book is called the Bible. God loves us *so much* that He doesn't want us to hurt ourselves or to hurt anyone else. He tells us what is right and what is wrong.

Miracles from God still happen today just like in the Bible. God continues to heal people and change their lives.

God puts people in your life to love you and guide you. There are so many wonderful things to learn. Obey your parents and listen to people who are wise and kind.

Sometimes people will hurt your feelings because they say or do unkind things. This makes God very sad because He wants you to be loved and taken care of. God tells us how to live a life pleasing to Him; but not everyone obeys Him. God sees our lives and cares about us in our happy times and in our sad times.

God wants you to talk to Him when you pray. He loves to spend time with you!

God is always with you, even when you feel afraid. When you are afraid or lonely, you can pray to God for courage and comfort. The Bible tells us, God will hear our cries and Jesus will come to us.

Sometimes even our friends will hurt us, but God always loves us. We can be alone but not be lonely, because He is with us.

God made you with a plan and a purpose for your life. He made you special and has something important for you to do.

The most important thing God wants you to do is to love Him and love other people. Sometimes that will be hard, but if you pray to God, He will help you learn how to love them.

God calls us His children. Even your mom and dad are His children.

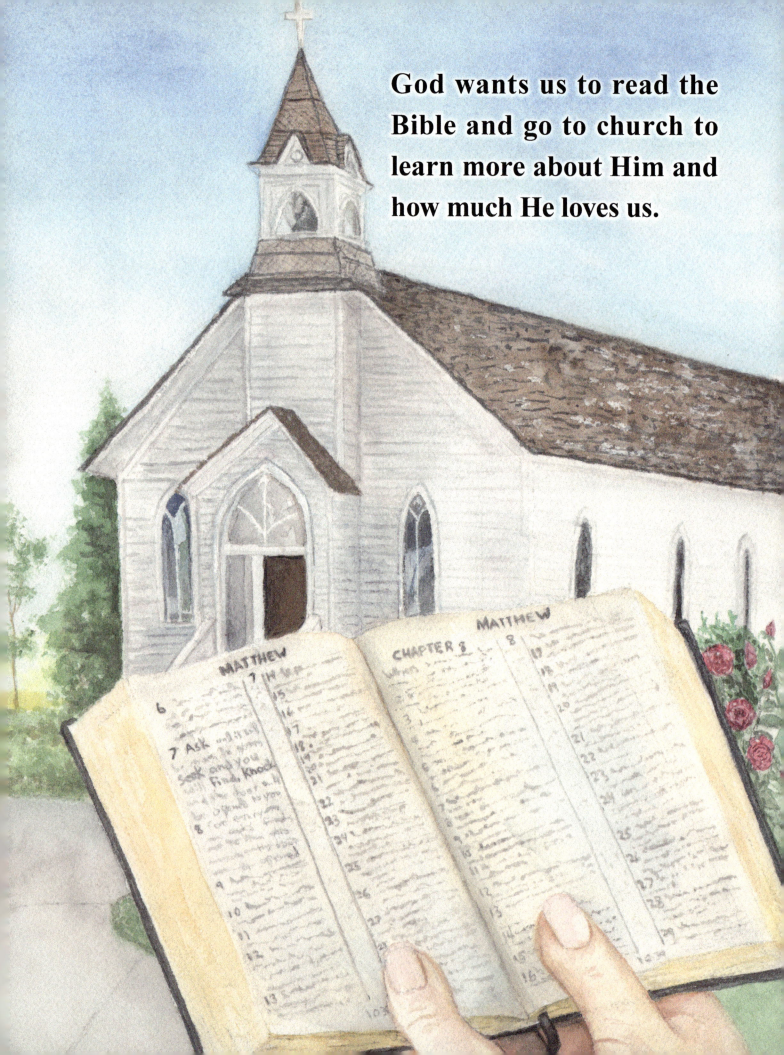

God wants us to read the Bible and go to church to learn more about Him and how much He loves us.

— A message from God just for you —

I love you *so much* that I sent My one and only Son, Jesus, to die for your sins (things you have done wrong).

— A message from God to you —

I love you *so much* that I want you to spend eternity with Me in heaven. Don't ever forget, I have always loved you and I always will!

Don't ever forget, God loves you!

**To learn more about God and how much
He loves you, please read the endnotes.**

Endnotes

[] Bracketed items were inserted by the author for clarification or definition.

Words printed in red are words spoken by Jesus.

Before you were born God loved you:

I knew you before I formed you in your mother's womb. (Jeremiah 1:5 NLT)

For You created my inmost being; You knit me together in my mother's womb. (Psalm 139:13)

For He chose us in Him before the creation of the world to be holy and blameless in His sight. In love He predestined us to be adopted as His sons through Jesus Christ, in accordance with His pleasure and will— to the praise of His glorious grace, which He has freely given us in the One He loves. (Ephesians 1:4–5)

The Lord appeared to us in the past, saying: "I have loved you with an everlasting love; I have drawn you with loving-kindness." (Jeremiah 31:3)

God watches over you:

From heaven the Lord looks down and sees all mankind; from His dwelling place He watches all who live on earth. (Psalms 33:13–14)

God put goodness inside you:

For everything God created is good, and nothing is to be rejected if it is received with thanksgiving, because it is consecrated [dedicated or set aside for God's purposes] by the word of God and prayer. (1 Timothy 4:4–5)

We have different gifts, according to the grace given us. (Romans 12:6)

For we are God's workmanship, created in Christ Jesus to do good works, which God prepared in advance for us to do. (Ephesians 2:10)

God put love inside you:

Now about brotherly love we do not need to write to you, for you yourselves have been taught by God to love each other. (1 Thessalonians 4:9)

And hope does not disappoint us, because God has poured out His love into our hearts by the Holy Spirit, whom He has given us. (Romans 5:5)

But God demonstrates His own love for us in this: While we were still sinners, Christ died for us. (Romans 5:8)

Dear friends, let us love one another, for love comes from God. Everyone who loves has been born of God and knows God. (1 John 4:7)

God put gifts and talents inside you:

We have different gifts, according to the grace given us. (Romans 12:6)

…each man has his own gift from God; one has this gift, another has that.

(1 Corinthians 7:7)

Every good and perfect gift is from above, coming down from the Father of the heavenly lights, who does not change like shifting shadows. (James 1:17)

Even twins are different:

See http://multiples.about.com/od/funfacts/a/differenttwins.htm for more information about twins.

God teaches us the way to live:

The Lord said to Moses, "Come up to me on the mountain and stay here, and I will give you the tablets of stone, with the law and commands I have written for their instruction." (Exodus 24:12)

The Lord commanded us to obey all these decrees [laws] and to fear the Lord our God, so that we might always prosper and be kept alive, as is the case today. (Deuteronomy 6:24)

… but I gave them this command; Obey Me, and I will be your God and you will be My people. Walk in all the ways I command you, that it may go well with you. (Jeremiah 7:23)

For this God is our God for ever and ever; He will be our guide even to the end. (Psalm 48:14)

God continues to do miracles:

You are the God who performs miracles; You display Your power among the nations. (Psalms 77:14)

This verse is still true here and now. In our lives today, God continues to perform miracles. People, who were told they would die, live active, healthy lives. People who were once mean, angry and abusive become loving.

> I will give you a new heart and put a new spirit in you; I will remove from you your heart of stone and give you a heart of flesh. (Ezekiel 36:26)

What is so amazing to me is that God can do anything and everything by Himself, but He wants us (you and me, all of us) to be part of His plan of love and redemption for His children. He allows us to be His hands and feet to love a hurting world. Jesus told us,

> "Very truly I tell you, whoever believes in Me will do the works I have been doing, and they will do even greater things than these, because I am going to the Father And I will do whatever you ask in My name, so that the Father may be glorified in the Son." (John 14:12–13)

With the permission of Pastor Johnny Zapara, I will tell you the story of a present day healing miracle. Pastor Zapara had attended a Vineyard Church Conference in 1984 and was skeptical when a lady who had been in a wheelchair for 5 years was healed and able to walk. The next few days he began to believe that the Holy Spirit of God was truly active and moving in their midst. He invited his mother, Norma, to attend with him the following day. When people were asked to come forward for prayer, he and his mother, who could barely move due to severe lupus and shingles, slowly moved to the area where people were being prayed for. He was disappointed when he saw a young man still in his teens move toward them. The young man came directly to his mother and asked what her problems were. The young man prayed and Pastor Zapara's mother was instantly and completely healed from both lupus and shingles. When the pastor moved his mother to live closer to him a few years later, standard tests were run by her new doctor and they went to the appointment to discuss them. The doctor said there seemed to be a discrepancy because her prior tests showed she had severe lupus. The doctor said her current blood work showed no signs of lupus. Pastor Zapara's mother said that was correct, she had been healed. The doctor said that was impossible. He said lupus could go into remission, but it is always detectable in the blood. Her blood work showed absolutely no signs of lupus. The pastor said, "That's correct. She had lupus, but she's healed." What the doctor didn't understand is what Jesus can do.

"Jesus looked at them and said, "With man this is impossible, but with God all things are possible." (Matthew 19:26)

In my own life I have experienced God so many times and in so many ways, so I have no doubt that God created us and the world, He loves us, and He wants to be a part of our lives every day. I have heard His voice, I have felt Jesus' presence and comfort, and daily the Holy Spirit guides my thoughts, words, and actions when I am willing to allow Him to lead me.

Obey your parents:

Listen, my son, to your father's instruction and do not forsake your mother's teaching. (Proverbs 1:8)

Children, obey your parents in everything, for this pleases the Lord.

(Colossians 3:20)

The quiet words of the wise are more to be heeded than the shouts of a ruler of fools. (Ecclesiastes 9:17)

Blessed is the man who finds wisdom, the man who gains understanding, for she [wisdom] is more profitable than silver and yields better returns than gold.

(Proverbs 3:13–14)

A kindhearted woman gains respect, but ruthless men gain only wealth.

(Proverbs 11:16)

Those who disregard discipline despise themselves, but the one who heeds correction gains understanding. (Proverbs 15:32)

He tends His flock like a shepherd; He gathers the lambs in His arms and carries them close to His heart; He gently leads those that have young. (Isaiah 40:11)

God is sad when someone hurts you:

"If anyone causes one of these little ones—those who believe in Me—to stumble, it would be better for them to have a large millstone hung around their neck and to be drowned in the depths of the sea." (Matthew 18:6)

God doesn't just get sad, he gets angry when people severely hurt you. Don't ever think someone gets away with doing something bad if they aren't caught. The Bible tells us that if those people don't feel bad about what they've done and ask for forgiveness, God will personally punish them.

God wants us to talk to Him:

> Do not be anxious about anything, but in every situation, by prayer and petition [asking for something], with thanksgiving, present your requests to God. And the peace of God, which transcends all understanding, will guard your hearts and your minds in Christ Jesus. (Philippians 4:6–7)

> Trust in Him at all times, you people; pour out your hearts to Him, for God is our refuge. (Psalm 62:8)

> Let us then approach God's throne of grace with confidence, so that we may receive mercy and find grace to help us in our time of need. (Hebrews 4:16)

God loves to spend time with us:

> For I am convinced that neither death nor life, neither angels nor demons, neither the present nor the future, nor any powers, neither height nor depth, nor anything else in all creation, will be able to separate us from the love of God that is in Christ Jesus our Lord. (Romans 8:38–39)

> You, Lord, are forgiving and good, abounding in love to all who call to You. (Psalm 86:5)

> The Lord appeared to us in the past, saying: "I have loved you with an everlasting love; I have drawn you with unfailing kindness. (Jeremiah 31:3)

God is always with you:

> Keep your lives free from the love of money and be content with what you have, because God has said, "Never will I leave you; never will I forsake you." So we say with confidence, "The Lord is my helper; I will not be afraid. What can mere mortals do to me?" (Hebrews 13:5–6)

When you are afraid, pray:

> When I am afraid, I put my trust in You. (Psalm 56:3)

When you lie down, you will not be afraid; when you lie down, your sleep will be sweet. (Proverbs 3:24)

God hears our cries:

A father to the fatherless, a defender of widows, is God in His holy dwelling. (Psalm 68:5)

Do not take advantage of a widow or an orphan. If you do and they cry out to Me, I will certainly hear their cry. My anger will be aroused, and I will kill you with the sword; your wives will become widows and your children fatherless.

(Exodus 22:22–24)

Jesus will come to us:

"I will not leave you as orphans; I will come to you." (John 14:18)

God has a plan and a purpose for your life:

Many, Lord my God, are the wonders You have done, the things You planned for us. None can compare with You; were I to speak and tell of Your deeds, they would be too many to declare. (Psalm 40:5)

For I know the plans I have for you," declares the Lord, "plans to prosper you and not to harm you, plans to give you hope and a future. (Jeremiah 29:11)

…for it is God who works in you to will and to act in order to fulfill His good purpose. (Philippians 2:13)

Love God and love others:

"Teacher, which is the greatest commandment in the Law?" Jesus replied: "Love the Lord your God with all your heart and with all your soul and with all your mind. This is the first and greatest commandment. And the second is like it: Love your neighbor as yourself. All the Law and the Prophets hang on these two commandments." (Matthew 22:36–40)

He will make it possible for you to love them:

May the Lord make your love for each other and for everyone else grow by leaps and bounds. That's how our love for you has grown. (1 Thessalonians 3:12 CEV)

Jesus looked at them and said, "With man this is impossible, but with God all things are possible." (Matthew 19:26)

God calls us His children if we choose to follow Him:

Do everything without grumbling or arguing, so that you may become blameless and pure, "children of God without fault in a warped and crooked generation." Then you will shine among them like stars in the sky. (Philippians 2:14–15)

This is how we know who the children of God are and who the children of the devil are: Anyone who does not do what is right is not God's child, nor is anyone who does not love their brother and sister. (1 John 3:10)

Study God's word and mature in His wisdom:

Fix these words of Mine in your hearts and minds; tie them as symbols on your hands and bind them on your foreheads. Teach them to your children, talking about them when you sit at home and when you walk along the road, when you lie down and when you get up. Write them on the doorframes of your houses and on your gates, (Deuteronomy 11:18–20)

And let us consider how we may spur one another on toward love and good deeds, not giving up meeting together, as some are in the habit of doing, but encouraging one another—and all the more as you see the Day approaching.

(Hebrews 10:24–25)

…because you know that the testing of your faith produces perseverance. Let perseverance finish its work so that you may be mature and complete, not lacking anything. If any of you lacks wisdom, you should ask God, who gives generously to all without finding fault, and it will be given to you. (James 1:3–5)

A message from God to you:

Many verses in the Bible tell us that God loves us and that His Son, Jesus, died to pay the price for the sins we have committed. The reason I write that this message is from God to you is because He woke me from a sound sleep to show me a vision of what these last 2 pages were to look like and what they should say. It was October 25th, 2013 in the early morning while it was still dark. God said to me, "Wake up, I have something to show you." I woke up to total darkness, so I closed my eyes to envision what God would show me. God said, "Open your eyes. I have something to show you." I looked up to the dark ceiling and immediately God showed me a bright, clear picture of this first page. It was SO bright that I was amazed it didn't wake my husband. God said, "On this page I want you to write, 'I love you *so much* that I sent my one and only Son, Jesus, to die for your sins'." Next God showed me the final page and said, "On this page I want you to write, 'I love you *so much* that I want you to spend eternity with Me in heaven'." I was so thrilled and humbled to know that God not only initiated the making of this book through the Holy Spirit, but He cared so much that He wanted to be sure that we all know that Jesus loved us so much that He took the punishment we deserved for the sins we have committed and died in our place. God doesn't just love us, He wants to spend time with us and give us wonderful and amazing gifts. Our time with Him in heaven begins here on earth as we learn about the heart of our heavenly Father and Creator. Our Father in heaven desires to have a relationship with us here and now, and for eternity. A relationship with God, Jesus and the Holy Spirit is far more loving and nurturing than any friendship, love or marriage we will experience on this earth. He is faithful to us even though we are often unfaithful to Him. If you haven't met or spent time with our Heavenly Father, start today. It is as simple as saying, "God, I thank you for creating the world and everyone in it, including me. Please help me to know You and accept Jesus as my Savior and the Lord of my life." The Bible tells us there is good and evil; and we need to choose God's right way of living to have the peace, joy and abundant life that He wants for each one of us.

The Bible tells us, "Come close to God, and God will come close to you. Wash your hands, you sinners; purify your hearts, for your loyalty is divided between God and the world." (James 4:8 NLT)

Jesus died to pay the price for our sins:

For God so loved the world that He gave his one and only Son, that whoever believes in Him shall not perish but have eternal life. (John 3:16)

"He himself bore our sins" in His body on the cross, so that we might die to sins and live for righteousness; "by His wounds you have been healed." (1 Peter 2:24)

God wants you to spend eternity with Him in heaven:

My sheep listen to My voice; I know them, and they follow Me. I give them eternal life, and they shall never perish; no one will snatch them out of My hand. My Father, who has given them to Me, is greater than all; no one can snatch them out of My Father's hand. (John 10:27–29)

So then, brothers and sisters, stand firm and hold fast to the teachings we passed on to you, whether by word of mouth or by letter. May our Lord Jesus Christ himself and

God our Father, who loved us and by His grace gave us eternal encouragement and good hope, encourage your hearts and strengthen you in every good deed and word. (2 Thessalonians 2:15–17)

Here is a trustworthy saying that deserves full acceptance: Christ Jesus came into the world to save sinners—of whom I am the worst. But for that very reason I was shown mercy so that in me, the worst of sinners, Christ Jesus might display His immense patience as an example for those who would believe in Him and receive eternal life. Now to the King eternal, immortal, invisible, the only God, be honor and glory for ever and ever. Amen. (1 Timothy 1:15–17)

(The apostle Paul wrote this to Timothy. Paul had once persecuted Christians [Paul had even watched with satisfaction as Stephen was stoned]; but Jesus opened Paul's heart to receive Him and the truth that Jesus was the long awaited Messiah who would save His people.)

But you, man of God, flee from all this, and pursue righteousness, godliness, faith, love, endurance and gentleness. Fight the good fight of the faith. Take hold of the eternal life to which you were called when you made your good confession in the presence of many witnesses. (1 Timothy 6:11–12)

Paul, a servant of God and an apostle of Jesus Christ to further the faith of God's elect and their knowledge of the truth that leads to godliness— in the hope of eternal life, which God, who does not lie, promised before the beginning of time, and which now at His appointed season He has brought to light through the preaching entrusted to me by the command of God our Savior, (Titus 1:1–3)

…whom He poured out on us generously through Jesus Christ our Savior, so that, having been justified by His grace, we might become heirs having the hope of eternal life. This is a trustworthy saying. And I want you to stress these things, so that those who have trusted in God may be careful to devote themselves to doing what is good. These things are excellent and profitable for everyone. (Titus 3:6–8)

How much more, then, will the blood of Christ, who through the eternal Spirit offered Himself unblemished to God, cleanse our consciences from acts that lead to death, so that we may serve the living God! For this reason Christ is the mediator of a new covenant, that those who are called may receive the promised eternal inheritance— now that He has died as a ransom to set them free from the sins committed under the first covenant. (Hebrews 9:14–15)

As for you, see that what you have heard from the beginning remains in you. If it does, you also will remain in the Son and in the Father. And this is what He promised us—eternal life. I am writing these things to you about those who are trying to lead you astray. (1 John 2:24–26)

Whoever believes in the Son of God accepts this testimony. Whoever does not believe God has made Him out to be a liar, because they have not believed the testimony God has given about His Son. And this is the testimony: God has given us eternal life, and this life is in His Son. Whoever has the Son has life; whoever does not have the Son of God does not have life. (1 John 5:10–12)

I write these things to you who believe in the name of the Son of God so that you may know that you have eternal life. This is the confidence we have in approaching God: that if we ask anything according to His will, He hears us. (1 John 5:13–14)

About the Author

Michele Hayes-Grisham has grown to love all God's children from the very young to the very old. When she began to pray to God to help her to see with His eyes, speak with His heart and become His hands and feet, new areas of service opened to her daily. She began to see others with a love and compassion she had never before known. At a church conference Michele learned that most of us who become Christians (85% of us) do so between the ages of 4 and 14*. However, most churches spend a relatively small percentage of their time, talents and resources to reach this age group. She was startled by this short window of openness to accept the love and peace that only Jesus can bring. It was then that the Holy Spirit whispered, "This is the reason why I want you to write another book." Michele had written her first book to encourage people not to give up when life seemed too hard to cope. Now she saw that a new challenge existed for her. It is extremely important that all children learn at an early age that there is a God who created them, loves them and has planned a way for them to live a life that is abundant. God gives our lives meaning while others who don't know Him feel hopeless and helpless. Michele and her husband, John, live in Shasta, California. They have one daughter in heaven and one on earth.

*For more original content like this, visit: http://home.snu.edu/~hculbert

About the Illustrator

"If what you are doing is not fruitful then you are probably not doing what God wants you to do." A few years ago, this saying helped me realize my focus was not in the right place. I said aloud that I wanted to use the gifts God gave me to be a blessing to Him and others with my art. Days later I was asked to do just that. Sometimes God whispers softly and sometimes He is loud and clear. God kept sending people to me with an artistic need and each time I answered His call, He would bring a bigger project. With each answer I was blessed and felt closer to God. It is a warm, wonderful feeling when you can see God working around you and even through you. I love God and feel called to serve Him and teach children about Him. I also feel as though God has called me to use my talents to be a blessing to Him and others.

> "Each one should use whatever gifts he has received to serve others, faithfully administering God's grace in its various forms. If anyone speaks, he should do it as one speaking the very words of God. If anyone serves, he should do it with the strength God provides, so that in all things God may be praised through Jesus Christ. To Him be the glory and the power forever and ever. Amen." (1 Peter 4:10–11)

Sheila Preston-Ford and her husband live in Anderson, California with their three children. She enjoys watercolor painting and is also an elementary art teacher at a Christian school.

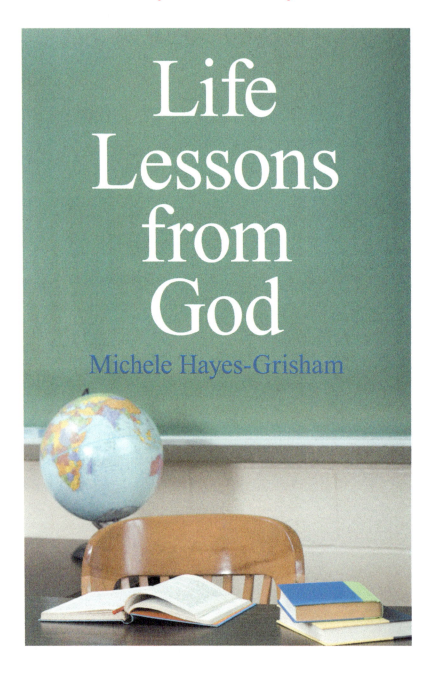

Life Lessons from God recounts Biblical as well as personal stories of how God uses everyday people like you and me to do His kingdom work. Don't accept a life without joy and peace. Jesus can teach you how to be His hands and feet in a hurting world. Your mission field is probably not around the world, but right in front of you. Go with God (Vaya con Dios)!

CPSIA information can be obtained
at www.ICGtesting.com
Printed in the USA
LVOW05s0416240218
567765LV00011BA/39/P